Shani Dev

Yantra Healing

GURU GAURAV ARYA

(Astrologer & Researcher)

Printed and bound in India

Title: Shani Dev Yantra Healing
Language: English

Guruweshvar
Publications

ISBN- 9788196821470

Table of Contents

About The Book

This book is written to give information about the Shani dev Yantra. But before knowing the Shani Yantra it is necessary to know about the Yantra, I mean simple Yantra.

Yantra (यन्त्र) (Sanskrit) (literally "Yantra, contraption" is a mystical diagram, mainly from the Tantric traditions of the Indian religions. They are used for the worship of deities in temples or at home; as an aid in meditation; used for the benefits given by their supposed occult powers based on Hindu astrology and tantric texts. They are also used for adornment of temple floors, due mainly to their aesthetic and symmetric qualities. Specific yantras are traditionally associated with specific deities. In the nine Planets, every planet have special Yantra, buy Shani yantra is useful in every manner. In this book, you will read how we can use the Shani yantra and how much this Yantra is effective and useful in Tantrik Tradition. I ll discuss also that Yantra is good to wear or should worship of Yantra in the home temple. Occult yantras are used as good luck charms, to ward off evil, as preventative medicine, in exorcism, etc., by using their magical power. When used as a talisman, the Yantra is seen to represent a deity who can be called on at will by the user. They are traditionally consecrated and energized by a priest, including the use of mantras which are closely associated to the specific deity and Yantra.

About the Author

Acharya Gaurav Arya is an Indian Astrologer and Researcher. He Is practicing in astrology since 2007. Now, After the completion of many cases, he is providing Astrological Services in the world.

He is an Indian Astrologer & Researcher. By profession, he is an Astrologer/Paranormal Expert and Occult master. At the beginning of Career he was a Mechanical Engineer after the completion of Engineering Projects he started Astrology Consulting. Now The Acharya Gaurav Arya is a leading name in Astrology. He wrote many books in the Hindi Language like "**Shree Shani Samhita**", "**Yantra Tatvam**".

Achievements- In 2017 Gaurav Arya awarded Jyotish Shree by CM of Uttarakhand and in 2018 he was awarded by Jyotish Vibhushan by CM of Uttarakhand, and in 2019 he was awarded and Award of Excellence in Astrology. Astrologer Gaurav Arya is Indian Paranormal Expert and occult master, he is regularly teaching Siddhi Sadhna to pupils.

He Gives Deeksha to their Pupils in every auspicious Day, for Blessings of Goddess Apsara, Bagalamukhi, Bhairav, Shani, Mahakali. He a is world known Vedic astrologer having expertise in all the departments of the Vedic astrology/Modern Occult Science/Paranormal Expertise. Working for the best of his Pupils, Gaurav Arya is practicing a range of services in Vedic as well as Occult Science/Paranormal Expertise from over the past 15 years. He has a supernatural vision to solve problems with all the ancient and modern capabilities. Either small or big, every problem has ended after meeting the eminent name in Astrology. Analyzing every problem deeply, he has the perfect resolution for everyone with the assistance of occult as well as simple astrological remedies. His services are unsurpassed with a wide variety of solutions available for all specific problems. Specialist of Yantra Development and Vedic Mantra and occult science remedy.

Acharya Gaurav Arya

Indian Astrologer & Researcher

Jyotish Shree, Jyotish Vibhushan, Paranormal Expert

Indian Mythologist, Spiritual Author.

THIS BOOK IS DEDICATED TO

MY GURU

TRIKAL DARSHI SHRI SHANI DEV

Introduction of Lord Shani Dev.

Shani Dev does not need any introduction because of Shani Dev makes fear for all sinners. I have no status, that I can tell about the Shani dev but due to my faith in Shani dev I am trying to tell about him.

Father of Lord Shani- **Surya Narayan**

Mother of Lord Shani- **Chadevi, Suvarna**

Shani Dev's brother- **Yamraj**

Shani Dev sister- **Yamuna Devi**

Shani Dev Guru- **Lord Shiva Shankar**

Birth Place- **Saurashtra, Gujarat**

Shani Dev Gotra- **Kashyap**

Complexion – **Dark Black**

Nature- **Tyagi, ascetic, vision, grumpy, serious, lucid.**

Friends- **Balaji, Hanumanji, Bhairav**

Other Names- **Chhayasut, Suryaputra, Konastha, Pingalo, Babhru, Raudratak, Sauri, Shanaichar, Krishnamand, Krishnau.**

Planet Friends- **Guru, Venus, Rahu, Mercury.**

Zodiac Friends- **Taurus, Gemini, Virgo, Libra**

Own Zodiac- **Capricorn, Aquarius**

Ownconstellation- **Pushya, Anuradha, Uttara-bhadrapada**

Area of Saturn- **Petroleum, iron, steel, industry, press, etc.**

Expertise- **Justice, Tantra, Punishment.**

Incarnation- **Lord Vishnu.**

Istha Devta**- Lord Krishna.**

By Nature- **Cruel and Kind**

What is yantra?

शरीरमिव जीवस्य दीपस्य स्नेःवत प्रिये ।

सर्वेषामपि देवानां तथा यन्त्रं प्रतिष्ठतम ॥

Lord Shiva tells Parvati that, O dear, just as the body is necessary for the live and oil is necessary for the lamp, similarly the Yantra is necessary for all the gods. Because "Yantram Devanam Gruham:" Yantra is the home of the gods. When Beej, numerals, etc. are written on the Yantra and then Yantra is awakened, then the power of the Yantra is created, which is the form of the deities, and proves the intended work. There are also Yantra shaktikars, that is, they succeed in shaktarma. The Yantra is used in Maran, vashikaran, elevation, astriction, etc.

Special Things about the Yantra

- Yantra are Easy to use.
- To get sucsess Yantra is best way
- Not Easy to cancel power of Yantra
- Yantra is equal to diety power.

- Just only Write Yantra can give you power or do your work.
- The procedure of Yantra is very easy.
- Yantra Never Failed.

The Word Yantra was born from "Yam" it means Metal. Here the meaning of this metal is Platform of Power who can generate power by the grace of God vision.

Meaning of Yantra and Designes.

Bindu

The central point of traditional yantras has a bindu or point, which represents the main deity associated with the Yantra. The retinue of the deity is often represented in the geometric parts around the center. The bindu in a yantra may be represented by a dot or small circle, or may remain invisible. It represents the point from which all of creation emanates. Sometimes, as in the case of the Linga Bhairavi yantra, the bindu may be presented in the form of a linga.

Triangle

Most Hindu yantras include triangles. Downward pointing triangles represent feminine aspect of God or Shakti; upward pointing triangles represent masculine aspect such as Shiva.

Hexagram

Hexagrams as shown in yantras are two equilateral triangles intertwined, representing the union of male and female aspects of divinity, or Shiva and Shakti.

Lotus

Mandalas and yantras both frequently include lotus petals, which represent purity and transcendence. Eight-petaled lotuses are common, but lotuses in yantras can include 2, 4, 8, 10, 12, 16, 24, 32, 100, 1000 or more petals.

Circle

Many mandalas have three concentric circles in the center, representing manifestation.

Outer square

Many mandalas have an outer square or nested squares, representing the earth and the four cardinal directions. Often they include sacred doorways on each side of the square.

Pentagram

Yantras infrequently use a pentagram. Some yantras of Guhyakali have a pentagram, due to the number five being associated with Kali.

Octagon

Octagons are also infrequent in yantras, where they represent the eight directions.

It has been said in the scriptures that no god is pleased unless Yantraj is worshiped. The Yantra is also a combination of the five elements. In which the elements representing fire element, air element, water element, earth element, sky element and all these elements are as follows.

Earth elements- (उ, ऊ, ओ, ग, ज, द, द, ब, ल।)
Water elements - (औ, घ, झ, द, ध, भा, व, स।)
Fire elements - (इ, ई, ऐ, ऐ, ख, छ, ठ, थ, फ, र।)
Air elements - (अ, आ, ए, क, च, त, त, प, य, ष।)
Sky element- (अ: अं, द, न्य, इ, न, म, श, ह)
According to the sum of the Yantra, the result is as follows.

The 15 yantra gives all kinds of accomplishment, and it is called Yantra Raj.

The Yantra of 16 destroys the obstruction of the thief etc.

The 19 Yantra works to prevent rotting.

20's Yantra is also a destroyer, eliminates all kinds of fear.

The 24's Yantra does not allow the target to hit properly.

The Yantra of 24 destroys the fear of disease.

The Yantra of 30 runs to Shakini.

The Yantra of 32 is used for delivery or at the time of birth of a child.

The Yantra of 34 is for might, eliminating all forms of fear.

The Yantra of 36 is useful for speculation.

The Yantra of 40 which gives respect of 40.

The Yantra of 50 stops crying.

The 58 Yantra is used in Vashikaran; Raja Vashikaran etc.

The Yantra of 62 Use for chils birth.

The 64 Yantra is ghost destroyer.

40 yantra gives courage.

42 give benefits in quarrels etc.

The Yantra of 6 is pleasing.

The 60 yantra is going to give Result of work.

The 65 yantra eliminates the crisis on the way.

90 end the rate of theft etc.

100 yantra is a wish fulfilling.

300 yantra is beneficial in regaining love.

400 yantra gives property.

Meaning of digits

0 Zero it represents God is not its direction.

1 This number represents perfection as well as karma, absolute, action.

2 This number represents the woman, as well as the water element.

3 This is the sum of the numbers 2 and 1, meaning it is made by combining these two. This device represents fulfillment.

अंक This number represents the earth and is dry.

5 This number represents man.

6 Displays additional content.

7 This number shows the rule.

8 This number represents infinite.

9 Demonstrates spirituality.

What is Shani Yantra?

Now we will talk about the Shani Yantra, What is shani Yantra in the below image we can see the Shani Yantra.

१२	७	१४
१३	११	९
८	१५	१०

In this Yantra the box size is 3x3 means there rows and three colunmns calling 3x3 Shani Yantra when we sum all the values of Row or Column we will get 33. So we can Say Shani Yantra Sum is 33 calling Yantra of 33. Shani Yantra can also bring a wide variety of benefits for the native who will depend on the general significances of Saturn, specific significances of Saturn in the horoscope of the native and the overall tone of the horoscope of the native.

Before knowing about the yantra values we should know how to Yantra works, in the below diagram we can see the Yantra have the following direction which is indicating the lord of direction. Every box of Yantra shows the place of god as shown in diagram. In the Img 1 the direction and their factors are showing. But in the Img2 4x4 box showing and in this box every box is indicating place of Angle like 1 cloumn and row box shows Ishan Kon (NE).

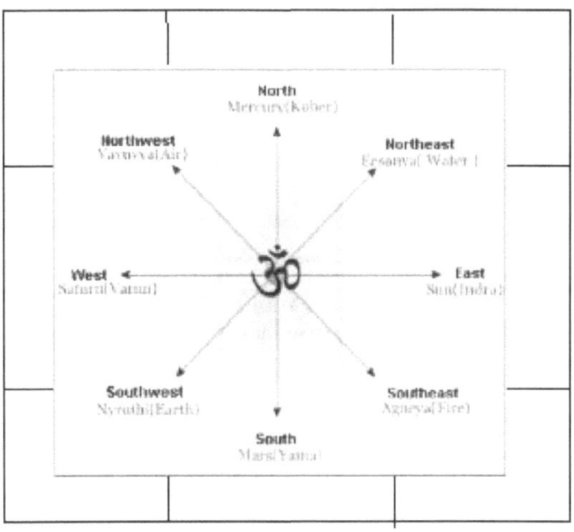

Img.1

Ishan		Agnaye
	Bharma	
Vayavya		Nratiya

Img.2

This diagram is fixing for every 4x4 box yantra. Now by using this diagram we will see the how shani Yantra working.

१२	७	१४
१३	११	९
८	१५	१०

In the yantra 12 Number shows the Guru Jupiter and 7 number shows the Venus and 14 number shows the Number of Sun and 13 number shows the number of moon and 11 number shows the shani and 9 number shows the guru Jupiter and 8 number shows the mars and 15 number shows the mercury and 10 number shows the shani.

In the ishan Kon (NE) angle Jupiter will give positive result and enhace the Ishan Angel (E). In the North Direction Venus will give good result. In the South East (Fire) here 14 number of sun shows the firing to balance. In the north direction 13 number shows the Moon and which balace the direction. In the centre 11 Number shows the Number of Saturn to energize the energy of Shani. And in the south direction 9 number is showing and this number shows the guru to balance the south. In the North West direction Number 8 and this number of mars and this number makes heavy to this direction to balance. In the west direction 15 numbers shows the mercury to heavy this side. And now in the South- West direction number of Rahu and Shani is showing here to balance. This method calling the Astrological planetry digit method.

This method is applicable only in 4x4 Yantra's who makes for 9 planets. In any other planets same formula will applicable.

Value of Shani Yantra

Shani Yantra is the Yantra of Lord Shani who is perceived to be the most aggressive deity due to which human fear of him while he is the most benevolent Lord at the core and does everything for the good of humankind as its only Shani Dev who could take the person at the highest mount or could make him stand at the lowest stand. Besides this, it is also the Yantra of planet Saturn which is ruled by the Lord Shani only. Mostly the value of Shani yantra is in nine Planets to remove the bad effects of Shani Dev. when we sum all digits of Shani yantra we will get 33 that's why this Yantra called Taitisa Yantra. The Shani yantra value is not simply its is very valuable Yantra to protect from Shani troubles in Sade satti. The Grid or Box Shani Yantra can be getting by this formula. As we Know the Surya Yantra is as follow.

6	1	8
7	5	3
2	9	4

As we know the Number system in Yantra

1. Moon
2. Mars
3. Mercury
4. Jupiter
5. Venus
6. Saturn
7. Rahu
8. Ketu

So if we need shani yantra then add 6 in row and column of Surya yantra. And as follow we can generate any yantra by using this folrmula. In the solar system Sun is the king in nine planets and every planet is moving around the sun.

12	7	9
13	11	9
8	15	10

So Sun yantra is making all Yantra as per system. In our solar system, the giant gas planets (Jupiter, Saturn, Uranus, and Neptune) spin more rapidly on their axes than the inner planets do and possess most of the system's angular momentum. The sun itself rotates slowly, only once a month. The planets all revolve around the sun in the same direction and in virtually the same plane. In addition, they all rotate in the same general direction, with the exceptions of Venus and Uranus. These differences are believed to stem from collisions that occurred late in the planets' formation. (A similar collision is believed to have led to the formation of our moon.)

As if we generate the Guru Yantra then we will add 4 in the surya yantra then will ger Guru Yantra or Jupiter Yantra.

6+4	1+4	8+4
7+4	5+4	3+4
2+4	9+4	4+4

10	5	12
11	9	7
6	13	8

In the above image we can see the Jupiter yantra.

Power of Shani Yantra

The power of Shani is can we measure by only using the Yantra in the opposite situation.

It is useful, when one feels depressed. It indicates sucess in wordly affairs, success in business and the man touches the dizzy heights. It is embossed on copper plate and is kept on rising moon Saturday during Venus or Saturn Hora. Shani yantra can not be failed in any situation. Shani have also many types of Yantra for diseases and wealth and negative energy. If seen originally the power of every Yantra in our trust. The right method of creating Yantra and his worship is the power of Yantra. Shani yantra can solve sade sati related issues, dhaya related issues can also solve. Shani yantra has the power to solve the problem in Shoes, petroleum-related issues. If we talk about the shani Yantra the 4x4 box shows the Yantra of 15 and this Yantra is useful to solve the obstacles.

The yantra is believed to harness the energy and influence of the planet Saturn and can have several potential benefits and powers:

1. **Protection from Saturn's Influence:** Lord Shani is often associated with challenging and karmic influences, and a Shani Yantra is used to mitigate the adverse effects of Saturn's position in one's birth chart. It is believed to protect individuals from the malefic aspects of Saturn and reduce its negative impact on their lives.

2. **Balancing Karmic Debts:** Saturn is thought to be the planet of justice and karma. A Shani Yantra is used to help individuals in resolving past karmic

debts and facing the consequences of their actions with patience and fortitude.

3. **Strengthening Discipline and Determination:** Lord Shani is associated with discipline and hard work. Meditating on or using a Shani Yantra can help individuals develop discipline, determination, and a strong work ethic to overcome challenges in life.

4. **Averting Obstacles:** Many people use the Shani Yantra to seek blessings for reducing obstacles, delays, and difficulties in their lives, including those related to career, health, and relationships.

5. **Promoting Spiritual Growth:** While Saturn is often associated with worldly challenges, it can also guide individuals

toward spiritual growth. The Shani Yantra is used to help individuals develop qualities like patience, endurance, and detachment, which are important in spiritual pursuits.

6. **Overall Well-Being:** Worship and meditation on the Shani Yantra are believed to promote overall well-being, mental peace, and harmony in life. It is said to reduce stress and anxiety.

7. **Professional Success:** For individuals seeking career success, the Shani Yantra can help them overcome professional obstacles and challenges, leading to growth and prosperity.

To harness the power of a Shani Yantra, it's important to establish a connection with it through regular worship, meditation, and mantra chanting. The specific benefits and experiences can vary from person to person, and it is essential to use the yantra with sincerity and devotion, understanding that it may help individuals in different ways based on their unique karmic situations and astrological influences.

How to Make Shani Yantra?

To Draw the Shani Yantra we have two methods First, make on Vedic method on Bhojpatra by using ashtagandha. The Second method makes Yantra on an iron plate or copper plate without any ink.

Method first- In this method takes a piece of Bhojpatra and make ashtagandha ink and write Yantra on bhojpatra by using the wooden stick Pomegranate.

As I mentioned above, the Ink is very important for the Yantra and it should be made with purity and this is the success of the Yantra.

Ashtagandha: which consists of eight types of elements like Kapoor, Agar, Tagar, Chandan, Kasturi, Turmeric, Keshar, Jatamasi Mixing in a certain proportion, liquefying the Ganges water and Gulab water creates the Asthgandha. Direction for Yantra when writing is West or east. Other method is as follow on solid materials

Steps to Make a Shani Yantra:

1. **Select a Metal Plate:** Choose a clean and purified piece of metal. Copper is commonly used, but you can use silver or gold if you prefer.

2. **Draw a Square:** Using a pencil and ruler, draw a square on the metal plate. The size of the square can vary, but it's typically between 3 to 6 inches on each side. Ensure that the lines are straight and the corners are right angles.

3. **Draw the Central Point:** Find the center of the square by drawing two diagonals. Where these diagonals intersect is the central point.

4. **Draw the Outermost Circle:** Use a compass to draw a circle inside the square, touching all four sides of the square.
5. **Draw Additional Circles:** Draw additional concentric circles within the first circle, each one smaller than the previous. Traditionally, there are seven circles, but the number may vary. These represent the orbits of Saturn's seven rings.
6. **Write the Mantra:** In the center of the Yantra, write the mantra associated with Lord Shani. The most common mantra is "ॐ शं शनैश्चराय नमः" (Om Sham Shanaischaraya Namah). Use red or black ink or paint for this. Write it in a clockwise direction starting from the top.

7. **Energize the Yantra:** Place the Yantra in your puja or meditation room. Light incense sticks and the lamp with ghee or oil. Recite the Shani mantra and offer prayers to Lord Shani while focusing on the Yantra. Imagine it being infused with divine energy.
8. **Regular Worship:** To maintain the power of the Yantra, it should be worshipped daily, especially on Saturdays, which are considered auspicious for Lord Shani. Light a lamp, offer incense, and recite the Shani mantra.
9. **Maintain Cleanliness:** Keep the Yantra and the area around it clean and pure. This is essential for the positive energy to flow effectively.

10. **Consult an Astrologer:** If you're making a Shani Yantra for astrological purposes, consider consulting an astrologer for guidance on how to use it effectively based on your birth chart.

Metals to Draw Yantra

You can draw Shani yantra on the iron plate or copper or Ashtadhatu plate after that energizes process is the same. Metal yantra should not wear in the neck because Yantra can harm to the neck. Pointed stick who will draw Yantra should also a same as drawing material.

Yantra can be draw by any machining process and after that can perform the energize process.

In the market many types of ready made Yantra's are available so before buy the Yantra should check the material. In many products printout are available on bhojpatra via printer that are totally wastages of money. These types of Yantra can not be energized and according to Vedic method this type of Yantra can not be activated. If you are drawing yantra self then it is good and now Yantra will give you effective results.

They can be drawn on various materials, including metals, to enhance their durability and longevity. Common metals used for drawing or engraving yantras include:

1. **Copper:** Copper is a popular choice for drawing yantras. It is believed to have special energy-conducting properties and is often used for its conductivity of electrical and spiritual energy.

2. **Silver:** Silver is considered a purer metal than copper and is used for yantras, especially when they are associated with goddesses or deities. Silver is believed to enhance the divine energy of the yantra.

3. **Gold:** Gold is a highly revered metal and is used for drawing yantras for

particularly powerful deities. It is believed to amplify the yantra's spiritual power.

4. **Brass:** Brass is a commonly used metal for yantra drawing due to its durability and cost-effectiveness. It conducts energy and is relatively easy to work with.
5. **Bronze:** Bronze is another option for creating yantras. It is a strong, durable alloy that can hold intricate designs.
6. **Aluminum:** While less traditional, aluminum is sometimes used for drawing yantras because it's lightweight, easy to work with, and resistant to corrosion.
7. **Steel:** Steel is another option, especially when long-lasting yantras are needed.

How to Energize Yantra

Worshiping the Yantra after the construction of the Yantra is as important as consuming water after the meal. By making the Yantra, the Yantra can be done by following the following method.

Purification

ॐ apvatra: pavitro wa sarvawastham gatoyapi wa yha Smreet Pundrikshakshan sha Bahyabhyantara: Shuchih.Pundrikshakshan Pundarikshakshan Pundarikshakshan

Take Ganga water in the right hand and purify all the ingredients then worship the land and mantra

Samudravasne Devi Parvatanamandite! Vishnupatni Namastubhayam Paadsparsham Kshaswame !!

And sprinkle the Ganges water

ॐ Prithvi! Tvaya dhrita loka Devi! Twam Vishnu Dhrita.Twinkle Mother Goddess! Holy Kuru Chasanam

Now say

- Om Keshvay Namah.
- Om Narayan.

Om Madhavaya Namah.(Sadhak should do a total of three achaanams)

ॐ Hridhekshai Namah. (Wipe the lips with the right-hand thumb origin)

ॐ Govinday Namah. (Wash your left hand)

Holy hold

(Wear the sacred ring or Kush, touch if the ring is from the first)

ॐ holy place Vaishnavya Saviturva: childbirth product Tasta te holypate holy puptya yatkamah pune tachhkeyam:

Take water in the right hand and recite the mantra and release the water

- ॐ Gram Devabhyo Namah (release water)
- ॐ ishta devatabhyo namah (release water)
- ॐ Kshetra Palayal Namah (release water)
- ॐ Kul Devatabhyo Namah (release water)
- ॐ Pitru Devatabhyo Namah (release water)
- ॐ Guru Devatabhyo Namah (release water)

Shani Yantra Effects

Shani yantra is mostly use to remove bad effects of Shani. Here Shani will improve the things which are related with the shani like Oil Industry, Asrology, Tantra Mantra, and Evil Effects. Shani Yantra is very effective in curtailing the malefic effects of planet Saturn. When Saturn is affecting you adversely or if you are under the influence of Sade Sati, using Shani Yantra proves beneficial. This Yantra is used to propitiate an afflicted Shani and helps tone down difficulties that you may be facing. When Saturn is malefic in a horoscope, in transit or causes Sadesati, use of Shani Yantra is very beneficial. Shani Yantra is useful, when one feels depressed. It indicates success in worldly affairs, success in business.

Here Shani Yantra will affect your Saturn In your birth chart. Shani yantra will effect to all direction of your life.

By the yantra effect if your Saturn is making problem in fisrt house then create Yantra and wear around neck.

If Shani is making problem in your second house then also wear it in neck

If shani is placed in 3rd house and making problem then place Yantra at your working place or in your worship room.

If shani is placed in 4th house and making problem then put this Yantra at your home.

If shani is placed in 5th house and making problem related to in study then wear it in your neck.

If shani is placed in 6th house and making problem then do not put Yantra at your home donate this Yantra into the shani mandir (temple).

If shani is placed in 7th house and making problem then wear it at your hand or do worship of Yantra.

If Shani is placed in 8th house and making problem then do not put it at your home put at any solitude place and do worship of at every Saturday.

If shani is placed in 9th house and making problem then shani yantra should placed in temple of house and do worship.

If shani is placed in 10th house and making problem then wear Yantra and do focus on your work.

If shani is placed in 11th house and making problem then wear it in neck or put at your working place.

If shani is placed in 12th house and making problem then put Yantra at any solitude place.

Rules to Wear or Worship of Yantra

Do not consume alcohol, unwanted sex means without love, do no take unwanted money. Do not take or give bribe.

Shani Yantra Uses

Shani Yantra use in Career

Yantra will improve Saturn related businesses.

1. It is very effective remedy for Shani Sade Satti, Shani Mahadasa.

2. It gives endurance, Power and Strength.

3. Makes ones thinking Rationale.

4. Balances the Mooladhara Chakra.

5. Give immense wealth and Properties.

6. Weak eyebrows

7. Ever had a problem due to fire

8. Fall of home/building

9. Accident with iron

10. Loss in construction work of building

Yantra's for Health

Here I am giving shani Yantra and other Yantra to cure some diseases.

Yantra for Epilepsy

४११२	४१११	२	७
६	३	४११३	४११५
४११८	४११३	८	१
४	५	४११४	४११७

Draw this Yantra on bhojpatra by using the wooden stick of chameli and then put it in silver locket and wear it in neck. After the completion of Yantra do worship of Yantra by using the chameli flowers.

Yantra for leprosy

In this disease, draw this shani Yantra on bojpatra and wear it in neck.

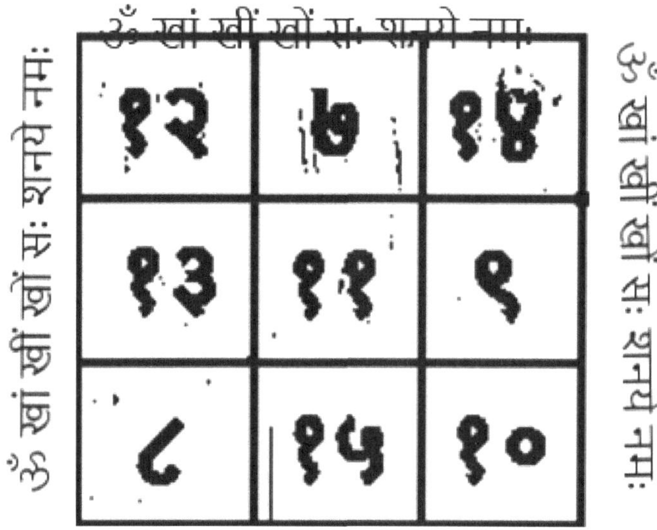

After the Yantra drawing complete then chant this mantra om Kham Kheem Khoom Sha Shanaye Namha 33 time and then do worship of shani by the help of Shree Shani Samhita Book and then Wear.

Yantra for Period Problems

This Yantra is very useful to remove all types of period problems in womens.

ह	१२५	२	५
१६	१०	१८	१९
अ	१०	१०	९९
१४०	३	३०	९९

Draw this Yantra on white paper via asthgandha and wear it in neck in a silver pendent.

Shani Yantra to Protection

शं	शं	शं	शं
शं	शं	शं	शं
शं	शं	शं	शं

Draw this Yantra at white paper by using the black ink and then wear it in neck after fiting into the silver pendent.

Yantra to Cure Small Pox

श्री	श्री	श्री
श्री	श्री	श्री
श्री	श्री	श्री

To draw this Yantra first we need to prepare the ink. Dip some raisins and kesar in a water for a night and then use this water to write the Yantra by using the Tulsi sitck. This Yantra should be prepared in Monday or Friday.

Shani Yantra's for Wealth

Lakshmi Yantra for wealth.

Draw this Yantra on bhojpatra with ashtgandh by using pomegranate wooden stick and then do worship of this Yantra by kheer (Milk+Rice Dish) and then do hawan for 108 days with this mantra "वं वं ह्रीं श्रीं क्लीं स्वाहा" and then wear Yantra in neck.

Note- To energize the yantra chant preem for 1000 times.

AsthLakshmi Sham Yantra

Draw this Yantra on bhojpatra by using the Gold nib/stick with asthganda and kesar paste on the day of Friday.

Do worship of Yantra by using the kheer or Sweets and also offer the red color flowers.

After the completion of Yantra do hawan with the following mantra 1108 times.

ॐ नमो आदेश गुरु का आदेश शनेश्वर महाराज का अष्टलक्ष्मी आगच्छ आगच्छ स्वाहा|

After this do worship of this yantra at every Saturday or Friday.

ShamGaj Yantra (शंगज यन्त्र)

This Yantra is very unique and not available in everywhere of tantra books, to prepare this Yantra we need a part of bhojpatra and draw this Yantra by using the ashtagandha with a wooden stick (as a pen) Chameli stick.

This Yantra should be drawn on Shukla Paksha Friday or Diwali. And then frame and keep at the worship place or working place.

Shani Yantra for Sade Sati

Sade-Sati is the 7 ½ years long period of (Shani). This astrological phase is much feared by those in India who believe Indian Astrology. This is a period with many challenges, but also a time of great achievements and recognition

Why Sade Sati duration is for 7.5 years?

Saturn is the planet which delays things and fructifies results, of your own efforts drawn at an earlier part of your life, very late. Shani takes 2.5 years to move from one sign to another sign of Zodiac Belt.

If we calculate it for 3 signs i.e. twelfth, first and second signs from the Natal Moon, it comes 3*2.5= 7.5 years. Let's understand how these 7.5 years are categorized in three phases or panoti during Saturn Transit:

Remedies for Sade Sati or Shani Dosha:

- Worshipping Lord Shani on every Saturdays is the best remedy ever to please Planet Saturn during Sade Sati.
- You can wear gemstone like Blue Sapphire after consulting with an Astrologer to reduce the malefic effects of Sade Sati.
- Reciting Hanuman Chalisa on daily basis can be helpful.
- Recite Shani Grah Mantra for 80,000 times.
- Wear an Iron ring in the middle finger of right hand, keep a note that it should be made out of horseshoe.
- Worship Lord Shiva by reciting "Siva Panchakshari" and Maha Mrityunjaya Mantra.

- Offer foods and things to the poor and needy people on Saturdays. Food items like Black Gram, Mustard Oil, Iron articles, black clothes, blanket, buffalo, money etc. should be donated.
- Offer copper, sesame oil to Saturn on every Saturdays.
- Pour Milk or Water on every Saturdays to please Saturn.
- Recite daily "Shani Stotram"
- Recite daily "Shani Kavacham"
- Feed grains and seeds to crows
- Feed honey and sugar to black ants.
- Donate curd rice to beggar and physically handicapped

Above are the remedies like initial treatment of Sade sati now, I would like to tell you some Yantra to reduce the bad effects of shani Sade sati.

Sade Sati Yantra

This Yantra should be drawn on the black cloth of cotton by using the iron nail with Chandan and then chant the following mantra.

om pram preem proum
shani shanicharya namha

<table>
<tr><td>३
५</td><td>३
७</td><td>३
५</td></tr>
<tr><td>३
७</td><td>३
५</td><td>३
७</td></tr>
<tr><td>३
५</td><td>३
७</td><td>३
५</td></tr>
</table>

After the completion of Yantra should wear in neck or shoulder. After the wearing, this Yantra should not consume alcohol or any other non-veg things.

Shani Yantra's for Enemy

Sometimes we face major problems due to the hidden type or on front enemies. In this section we will learn major types of shani yantra's.

Shani Yantra to defate enemy.

Draw this Yantra on bhojpatra on the day of Saturday with asthgandha or any other types of ink by using the wooden stick of pomegranate.

After this wear this Yantra on neck or keep inside your home or wallet.

Note- Do not uses this Yantra for innocent person otherwise Yantra will defeat the owner. This Yantra also can use to remove negative energy from body of anyone or from anyplace.

Shani Yantra to kill Enemy

33	33	33	33	33
33	33	33	33	33
33	33	33	33	33
33	33	33	33	33

Draw this Yantra on bhojpatra on the day of Saturday with asthgandha or any other types of ink by using the wooden stick of pomegranate.

After this wear this Yantra on neck or keep inside your home or wallet.

Note- Do not uses this Yantra for innocent person otherwise Yantra will defeat the owner.

108 Mantra of Shani Dev

१. ॐ शनैश्चराय नमः

२. ॐ शनैश्चारय नमः

३. ॐ मन्दये नमः

४. ॐ पिप्पलाय नमः

५. ॐ आरकाय नमः

६. ॐ शौरये नमः

७. ॐ वक्रतुण्डाय नमः

८. ॐ नीलाय नमः

९. ॐ कृष्णाय नमः

१०. ॐ श्यामाय नमः

११. ॐ काकाय नमः

१२. ॐ पिप्पलाय नमः

१३. ॐ उग्राय नमः

१४. ॐ भास्कराय नमः

१५. ॐ गोदाय नमः

१६. ॐ यमाय नमः

१७. ॐ आरुषाये नमः

१८. ॐ वक्रतुण्डाय नमः

१९. ॐ शनिकीर्तये नमः

२०. ॐ क्रूराय नमः

२१. ॐ तीक्ष्णाय नमः

२२. ॐ धराय नमः

२३. ॐ यमपुत्राय नमः

२४. ॐ महाकालाय नमः

२५. ॐ शनैश्चराय नमः

२६. ॐ शनैश्चारय नमः

२७. ॐ मन्दये नमः

२८. ॐ पिप्पलाय नमः

२९. ॐ आरकाय नमः

३०. ॐ शौरये नमः

३१. ॐ वक्रतुण्डाय नमः

३२. ॐ नीलाय नमः

३३. ॐ कृष्णाय नमः

३४. ॐ श्यामाय नमः

३५. ॐ काकाय नमः

३६. ॐ पिप्पलाय नमः

३७. ॐ उग्राय नमः

३८. ॐ भास्कराय नमः

३९. ॐ गोदाय नमः

४०. ॐ यमाय नमः

४१. ॐ आरुषाये नमः

४२. ॐ वक्रतुण्डाय नमः

४३. ॐ शनिकीर्तये नमः

४४. ॐ क्रूराय नमः

४५. ॐ तीक्ष्णाय नमः

४६. ॐ धराय नमः

४७. ॐ यमपुत्राय नमः

४८. ॐ महाकालाय नमः

४९. ॐ सूर्यपुत्राय नमः

५०. ॐ छायापुत्राय नमः

५१. ॐ धरापुत्राय नमः

५२. ॐ यमपुत्राय नमः

५३. ॐ कालकालाय नमः

५४. ॐ महात्मने नमः

५५. ॐ लोकधराय नमः

५६. ॐ दुखहन्त्रे नमः

५७. ॐ मन्दचापाये नमः

५८. ॐ जयाय नमः

५९. ॐ दंडहस्ताय नमः

६०. ॐ क्षपाय नमः

६१. ॐ क्रूरविक्रामाय नमः

६२. ॐ मंदरध्वजाय नमः

६३. ॐ मंदराय नमः

६४. ॐ क्षितिपतये नमः

६५. ॐ वक्रदृशाये नमः

६६. ॐ कपिलाय नमः

६७. ॐ शनिध्वजाय नमः

६८. ॐ शनिमण्डलाये नमः

६९. ॐ शनये नमः

७०. ॐ काकसुताय नमः

७१. ॐ पिप्पलादाये नमः

७२. ॐ मंदविक्रमाय नमः

७३. ॐ धरणिपतये नमः

७४. ॐ धरणिप्रियाये नमः

७५. ॐ सनकराये नमः

७६. ॐ सूर्यछायाये नमः

७७. ॐ महाकालाय नमः

७८. ॐ वक्रद्दशे नमः

७९. ॐ शनिप्रियाये नमः

८०. ॐ शनैश्चराये नमः

८१. ॐ मंदराय नमः

८२. ॐ धरणिभयाये नमः

८३. ॐ लोकपूज्याये नमः

८४. ॐ दुखनाशाये नमः

८५. ॐ पिप्पलादाये नमः

८६. ॐ वक्रद्दशे नमः

८७. ॐ धरणिपालाये नमः

८८. ॐ प्रभवाये नमः

८९. ॐ विद्याधराये नमः

९०. ॐ नित्यशनये नमः

९१. ॐ क्रूरछायाये नमः

९२. ॐ शनिप्रियाये नमः

९३. ॐ शनिध्वजाये नमः

९४. ॐ शनिमण्डलाये नमः

९५. ॐ शनये नमः

९६. ॐ काकसुताये नमः

९७. ॐ पिप्पलादाये नमः

९८. ॐ मंदविक्रमाय नमः

९९. ॐ धरणिपतये नमः

१००. ॐ धरणिप्रियाये नमः

१०१. ॐ सनकराये नमः

१०२. ॐ सूर्यछायाये नमः

१०३. ॐ महाकालाय नमः

१०४. ॐ वक्रद्दशे नमः

१०५. ॐ शनिप्रियाये नमः

१०६. ॐ शनैश्चराये नमः

१०७. ॐ मंदराय नमः

१०८. ॐ धरणिभयाये नमः

Certainly, here's the text provided in Romanized Sanskrit:

1. ***Om Shanaishcharaya Namah***
2. ***Om Shanaischaraya Namah***
3. ***Om Mandaya Namah***
4. ***Om Pippalaya Namah***
5. ***Om Arakaya Namah***
6. ***Om Shauraye Namah***
7. ***Om Vakra-Tundaya Namah***
8. ***Om Neelaya Namah***
9. ***Om Krishnaaya Namah***
10. ***Om Shyamaya Namah***
11. ***Om Kakaya Namah***

12. Om Pippalaya Namah

13. Om Ugra-Ya Namah

14. Om Bhaskaraya Namah

15. Om Godaya Namah

16. Om Yamaya Namah

17. Om Arushaye Namah

18. Om Vakra-Tundaya Namah

19. Om Shani-Kirtaye Namah

20. Om Krura-Ya Namah

21. Om Teekshnaaya Namah

22. Om Dharaaya Namah

23. Om Yama-putraya Namah

24. Om Maha-kaalaya Namah

25. Om Shanaishcharaya Namah

26. Om Shanaischaraya Namah

27. Om Mandaya Namah

28. Om Pippalaya Namah

29. Om Arakaya Namah

30. Om Shauraye Namah

31. Om Vakra-Tundaya Namah

32. Om Neelaya Namah

33. Om Krishnaaya Namah

34. Om Shyamaya Namah

35. Om Kakaya Namah

36. Om Pippalaya Namah

37. Om Ugra-Ya Namah

38. Om Bhaskaraya Namah

39. Om Godaya Namah

40. Om Yamaya Namah

41. Om Arushaye Namah

42. Om Vakra-Tundaya Namah

43. Om Shani-Kirtaye Namah

44. Om Krura-Ya Namah

45. Om Teekshnaaya Namah

46. Om Dharaaya Namah

47. Om Yama-putraya Namah

48. Om Maha-kaalaya Namah

49. Om Surya-putraya Namah

50. Om Chaya-putraya Namah

51. Om Dhara-putraya Namah

52. Om Yama-putraya Namah

53. Om Kaala-kaalaya Namah

54. Om Mahatmane Namah

55. Om Loka-dharaaya Namah

56. Om Dukha-hantri Namah

57. Om Manda-chapaye Namah

58. Om Jaya-namah

59. Om Danda-hastaaya Namah

60. Om Kshapaya Namah

61. Om Krura-vikramaaya Namah

62. Om Mandara-dhwajaaya Namah

63. Om Mandaraaya Namah

64. Om Kshitipatiyaya Namah

65. Om Vakra-drishaye Namah

66. Om Kapilaaya Namah

67. Om Shani-dhwajaaya Namah

68. Om Shani-mandalaaya Namah

69. Om Shanaye Namah

70. Om Kaka-sutaaya Namah

71. Om Pippladaaya Namah

72. Om Manda-vikramaaya Namah

73. Om Dharani-pate Namah

74. Om Dharani-priyaya Namah

75. Om Sana-karaya Namah

76. Om Surya-chhayaaya Namah

77. Om Maha-kaalaya Namah

78. Om Vakra-drishe Namah

79. Om Shani-priyaaya Namah

80. Om Shanaishcharaaya Namah

81. Om Mandaraaya Namah

82. Om Dharani-bhaya Namah

83. Om Lokapujyaya Namah

84. Om Dukha-nashaaya Namah

85. Om Pippladaaya Namah

86. Om Vakra-drishe Namah

87. Om Dharani-paalaaya Namah

88. Om Prabhavaaya Namah

89. Om Vidya-dharaya Namah

90. Om Nitya-shaniaya Namah

91. Om Krura-chhayaaya Namah

92. Om Shani-priyaaya Namah

93. Om Shani-dhwajaaya Namah

94. Om Shani-mandalaaya Namah

95. Om Shanaaye Namah

96. Om Kaka-sutaaya Namah

97. Om Pippladaaya Namah

98. Om Manda-vikramaaya Namah

99. Om Dharani-pate Namah

100. Om Dharani-priyaya Namah

101. Om Sana-karaya Namah

102. Om Surya-chhayaaya Namah

103. Om Maha-kaalaya Namah

104. Om Vakra-drishe Namah

105. Om Shani-priyaaya Namah

106. Om Shanaishcharaaya Namah

107. Om Mandaraaya Namah

108. Om Dharani-bhaya Namah

Shani Kavcham

शनि कवचं

अथ श्री शनिकवचम्

अस्य श्री शनैश्चरकवचस्तोत्रमंत्रस्य कश्यप ऋषिः ॥

अनुष्टुप् छन्दः ॥ शनैश्चरो देवता ॥ शीं शक्तिः ॥

शूं कीलकम् ॥ शनैश्चरप्रीत्यर्थं जपे विनियोगः ॥

निलांबरो नीलवपुः किरीटी गृध्रस्थितस्त्रासकरो धनुष्मान् ॥

चतुर्भुजः सूर्यसुतः प्रसन्नः सदा मम स्याद्वरदः प्रशान्तः ॥ १ ॥

ब्रह्मोवाच ॥

श्रुणूध्वमृषयः सर्वे शनिपीडाहरं महत् ।
कवचं शनिराजस्य सौरेरिदमनुत्तमम् ॥ २ ॥

कवचं देवतावासं वज्रपंजरसंज्ञकम् ।
शनैश्चरप्रीतिकरं सर्वसौभाग्यदायकम् ॥ ३ ॥

ॐ श्रीशनैश्चरः पातु भालं मे सूर्यनंदनः ।
नेत्रे छायात्मजः पातु पातु कर्णौ यमानुजः ॥ ४ ॥

नासां वैवस्वतः पातु मुखं मे भास्करः सदा ।

स्निग्धकंठःश्च मे कंठं भुजौ पातु महाभुजः ॥ ५ ॥
स्कंधौ पातु शनिश्चैव करौ पातु शुभप्रदः ।
वक्षः पातु यमभ्राता कुक्षिं पात्वसितत्सथा ॥ ६ ॥
नाभिं ग्रहपतिः पातु मंदः पातु कटिं तथा ।
ऊरू ममांतकः पातु यमो जानुयुगं तथा ॥ ७ ॥
पादौ मंदगतिः पातु सर्वांगं पातु पिप्पलः ।
अङ्गोपाङ्गानि सर्वाणि रक्षेन्मे सूर्यनंदनः ॥ ८ ॥
इत्येतत्कवचं दिव्यं पठेत्सूर्यसुतस्य यः ।
न तस्य जायते पीडा प्रीतो भवति सूर्यजः ॥ ९ ॥
व्ययजन्मद्वितीयस्थो मृत्युस्थानगतोऽपि वा ।
कलत्रस्थो गतो वापि सुप्रीतस्तु सदा शनिः ॥ १० ॥
अष्टमस्थे सूर्यसुते व्यये जन्मद्वितीयगे ।
कवचं पठतो नित्यं न पीडा जायते क्वचित् ॥ ११ ॥
इत्येतत्कवचं दिव्यं सौरेर्यनिर्मितं पुरा ।
द्वादशाष्टमजन्मस्थदोषान्नाशायते सदा ।
जन्मलग्नास्थितान्दोषान्सर्वान्नाशयते प्रभुः ॥ १२ ॥

॥ इति श्रीब्रह्मांडपुराणे ब्रह्म–
नारदसंवादें शनैश्चरकवचं संपूर्ण ॥

Shani Kavacham

Atha Shri Shanikavacham.

Asya Shri Shanaishcharakavachastotramantrasya Kashyap Rishi II Anushtubh Chhandah II Shanaishcharo Devata II Sheem Shaktih II Shoom Keelakam II Shanaishcharapreetyartham Jape Viniyogah II Nilaambaro Neelavapuh Kireetee Grudhrasthitastrasakaro Dhanushman Chaturbhujah Suryasutah Prasannah Sada Mama Syadvardhah Prashantah 1

Brahmovacha II

Shrunudhvamrishayah Sarve Shanipidaharam Mahat I Kavacham Shanirajasya Saureridam Anuttamam 2

Kavacham Devatavasam Vajrapanjarasamjnakam I Shanaishcharapreetikaram Sarvasaubhagyadayakam 3

Om Shree Shanishcharah Patu Bhalam Me
Suryanandana I Netre Chhayatmajah Patu Patu
Karnau YamAnujah 4

Nasam Vaivaswatah Patu Mukham Me Bhaskarah
Sada I Snigdhakanthah Shcha Me Kantham Bhujau
Patu Mahabhujah 5

Skandhau Patu Shanishchaiva Karau Patu
Shubhapradah I Vakshah Patu Yamabhrata
Kukshim Patvastatsatha 6

Nabhim Grahapatih Patu Mandah Patu Katim Tatha
I Ooru Mamantakah Patu Yamo Januyugam Tatha
7

Paadau Mandagatih Patu Sarvangam Patu Pippalah
I Angopangaani Sarvaani Rakshenme Suryanandana
8

Ityetat Kavacham Divyam Pathetsuryasutasya Yah I
Na Tasya Jayate Peedaa Preeto Bhavati Suryajah 9

Vyayajanmadviteeyastho Mrityusthaanagato'spi

Vaa I Kalatrastho Gato Vaapi Supreetastu Sadaa

Shanih 10

Ashtamasthe Suryasute Vyaye Janmadviteeyage I

Kavacham Pathato Nityam Na Peedaa Jayate

Kvachit 11

Ityetat Kavacham Divyam Saureryanirmitam Pura I

Dwadashashtamajanmasthadoshannaashayate Sadaa

12

Iti Shree Brahmanda Purane

Brahmanaaradasamvaade

Shanishcharakavacham Sampurnam